WORLD CLASS SMILES, MADE IN DETROIT

WORLD CLASS SMILES, MADE IN DETROIT

The Straight-Shooting Orthodontist's
Guide to Your Amazing Smile

Jamie Reynolds DDS, MS

Diplomate, American Board of Orthodontics

ISBN: 1530355583
ISBN 13: 9781530355587
Library of Congress Control Number: 2016904027
CreateSpace Independent Publishing Platform
North Charleston, South Carolina

Thoughts on Dr. Reynolds and his new book,
World-Class Smiles, Made in Detroit

I have had the good fortune to meet thousands of clinicians worldwide and can honestly say that I put Dr. Reynolds in a special group of very elite clinicians. His passion to continually improve the final results for his patients is so very impressive and should be emulated by all clinicians. The highest recommendation I can give any clinician is to say that I would drive many miles to have any family member treated by Dr. Reynolds. Patients are very fortunate when they are the beneficiary of such high quality orthodontic care.

Dr. Dwight Damon
Spokane, WA

I have known Dr. Reynolds for over 10 years now. I can honestly say that he is amongst the highest caliber orthodontists in the world. If there was an authority in Orthodontics, he is your guy. Dr. Reynolds has never strayed from the standards of clinical excellence that so many doctors fall short of. He exhibits passion for the profession and is always on the side of the consumer. I am thrilled to offer this resource to my patients in Colorado. Thank you, Dr. Reynolds. You are a role model to all of us as an author, orthodontist, husband, and father.

DR. ANIL IDICULLA
DENVER, COLORADO

Dr. Reynolds is an inspiration to orthodontists throughout the world.

His experience, skill, and dedication to ever improving the field of orthodontics is renowned. Dr. Reynolds is always at the forefront of using the latest proven technologies to the benefit of his patients. Jamie generously shares his knowledge lecturing nationally and internationally, setting the benchmark for the highest quality of orthodontic care.

DR. ASHLEY T. SMITH
TOOWOOMBA
QUEENSLAND, AUSTRALIA

As an orthodontist who lectures worldwide, I've had the opportunity to meet many orthodontists. Few orthodontists stand out like Dr. Reynolds. I've seen the smiles he creates and love how he combines new technology with a personal touch to make a difference to every patient under his care. If you're looking for an orthodontist anywhere in the Detroit area, his office would be my first choice!

DR. JEFF KOZLOWSKI
NEW LONDON, CONNECTICUT

I've had the good fortune of knowing Dr. Reynolds for a long time now, and he is an extraordinary clinician. He has an artist's eye and treats his patients with kindness. Dr. Reynolds truly makes me proud to share the profession with him. He has my highest possible recommendation.

JOHN GRAHAM, DDS, MD
SALT LAKE CITY, UTAH

Dr. Reynolds is an orthodontist that a fellow orthodontist would send their own children to for treatment! I have had the pleasure of knowing his amazing team for many years now. We have had numerous interactions and opportunities to think, create, and progress the profession in ways that we never thought possible ten years ago. It is through these professional interactions that I can honestly say there is no finer or more ethical team of clinical orthodontists. You can always trust Dr. Reynolds and his team to present the right treatment for you or your child.

Dr. Jep Paschal
Madison, Georgia

I am a local dentist and have had all three of my children and my wife treated by Dr. Spillane and Dr. Reynolds. Having a professional background in dentistry, I have a better understanding of how people's teeth should fit together to get an optimal bite and aesthetic. I also could have sent my family to many other orthodontic offices, but I sent them to this office because I believe they provide the best orthodontic treatment in the area. All had exceptional outcomes and had fun at their office while under their care. Highly recommend this office for all your orthodontic needs.

Dr. David Salah
Novi, Michigan

I have interacted with orthodontists across the United States. Dr. Reynolds stands out as the cream of the crop. His office takes great care of their patients and produce excellent results. When you trust your smile to Spillane & Reynolds, you are making a great decision. You also get to know an entire team of fantastic people!

DR. BECKY SCHREINER
ST. LOUIS, MISSOURI

When I refer our patients for orthodontic care, it has to be where I would send my family. This is the office I send my family! Dr. Spillane and Dr. Reynolds are committed to providing their patients with the highest level of service and care through advanced technology, education, outstanding facility, and a great team. Thank you for providing our patients with the best in orthodontic care! I appreciate all the excellent communication in coordinating treatment for our patients.

You are the best!

DR. JAMES C. ROSS
NOVI, MICHIGAN

As an orthodontic professional, I often look to Dr. Spillane and Dr. Reynolds as role models for my practice and my personal life. They continually exceed my expectations as professionals with their exceptional care, attention to detail, and never-ending quest to improve their office and treatment. I have found their first priority is their patients. We do not always find this to be true in today's busy world, but they never cease to amaze me. Their goal is to take care of the patient first. Whether that means the exceptional care they give their patients or their consistent search for knowledge through continuing education, they focus on what is truly important: the PATIENT. If my children were being treated by another orthodontist, Dr. Reynolds and Dr. Spillane would be my choice!

Dr. Anthony Harwell
Amarillo, Texas

I am fortunate to belong to a national study club with Dr. Reynolds. He is quick to offer insightful ideas to treat a wide variety of cases. This willingness to share enhances the quality of care I can deliver to my own patients. His commitment to quality orthodontic treatment results, exceptional service to his patients, and early adoption of the latest technology are the qualities that I strive to emulate in my own practice.

Dr. Rob Sheffield
Antioch, California

There are moments in life when you cross paths with friends and colleagues and realize that they are making a difference in people's lives. I have had the good fortune to be introduced to Dr. Reynolds at the University of Michigan. As a doctor he is on the leading edge and provides the highest quality treatment for his patients. He continues to embark on improving his patients' experience, reduce treatment time, and provide the highest quality of treatment that every patient deserves. As a colleague, I have had the opportunity to improve my own clinical attributes with the help and guidance of Dr. Reynolds. I am truly fortunate and thankful to have the opportunity to share *a professional and personal friendship with this amazing doctor.*

DR. DEREK STRAFFON
DENVER, COLORADO

As a dentist, parents are always asking me how to find the right orthodontist. They usually rely on my suggestions, but with this book they will be better informed and know the right questions to ask. This book is easy for parents and patients to understand and really provides great insight in finding your perfect smile maker!

DR. CHARLOTTE KROLL
ROCHESTER HILLS, MICHIGAN

Dr. Reynolds, a colleague whom I admire and respect, has written a common sense, easy to understand description of the world of orthodontics. This book is a must read for anyone considering orthodontic treatment so they can better understand their options and learn from one of the best in the field

DR. MIKE GOLDSTEIN
TORONTO, CANADA

I was fortunate to meet Dr.Reynolds several years ago lecturing at a Insignia customized digital orthodontics core users meeting. I was immediately taken by his wonderfully treated cases, his knowledge and his graceful attitude. I am proud to be his friend and always recommend his courses to fellow orthodontists who strive for excellence!"

Dr. Nimet Guiga
Cascais, Portugal

My Bubba
My Angel
My Monkey
My Wife

My Inspiration
My Dreams
My Purpose
My Life

For my family and their uncompromising support of my many endeavors.

Contents

My Story · 1

How to Choose Your Best Provider· · · · · · · · · · · · · · · · · 9

Why Should I Care about My Bite? · · · · · · · · · · · · · · · 23

Does My Seven-Year-Old Really Need Braces? · · · · · · 31

Think Twice before Having Permanent
Teeth Removed · 47

How to Get a Beautiful Smile without
Being a "Metal Mouth" · 53

Accelerating Treatment· 63

How to Make Orthodontic Treatment Affordable · · · · 81

Eleven Things Parents Should Consider When
Choosing an Orthodontist · 87

My Story

*All the secrets of the world are contained
in books. Read at your own risk.*

—LEMONY SNICKET

First, thank you for picking up this book. With all the information available for an orthodontic consumer in an ever-changing world, the choices of care for you and your loved ones are ever expanding. Frankly, if I were currently looking for straighter teeth or a healthier bite, my head would spin as I considered all the options. This realization got me thinking that maybe I could help clear some of the fog and create an easy-to-read orthodontic guide that is informative and hopefully a little fun. My goal for this book is to provide the orthodontic consumer with easy-to-understand, no-nonsense information about orthodontics that is in line with the best techniques available today.

Second, I wanted to extend personal thanks to the people who make up the images displayed in this book. All of the photos, including the cover, are patients of our practice. It gives me great pride to see their smiles displayed in the pages of this book.

Here's a little background on me: I grew up in Lake Orion, Michigan, with my wonderful parents, Bob and Jane Reynolds. Dad was a phone-company employee, and, up until her retirement when my sister, Erin, was born, Mom was a special-education teacher for blind children. Lake Orion was, at the time, home to the largest factory under one roof in the world. Since Lake Orion is a suburb of Detroit, it shouldn't be much of a surprise that the factory made cars (and still does to this day). My sister and I grew up in a loving family and community that valued education and taught us the value of hard work, honesty, and integrity.

I grew up a sports-obsessed kid who desperately dreamed he was the Irish equivalent of local basketball hero Isiah Thomas. My daily wardrobe consisted of anything I had with *Detroit Pistons* on it. Sadly, my crossover dribble was not NBA caliber, and my basketball career ended with my high-school career. I went to college planning to become an athletic trainer and majored in exercise physiology. I wanted to be as close to sports as possible in my work. A friend talked me into trying out for the University of Michigan men's volleyball team, and we were both shocked when I made the final spot on the roster without having had any organized volleyball experience. As it turns out, some basketball skills do cross over into volleyball. Over the next several seasons, I went on to become team captain and to garner all–Big Ten and all-region honors. Following college, my volleyball obsession headed me to the sand and the pro beach two-on-two sand volleyball circuit. If you have never been to the Midwest, you may not know that it has some fantastic beaches—believe it or not. In fact, the beaches along the Lake Michigan shore are some of the best in the world, and they are chock-full of talented volleyball players. I took my shot at the AVP tour—the NBA of beach volleyball—but, as it turned out, I found a day job that trumped my passion for the beach (for the most part—I still find my way to the beach as often as possible). Along the way, I did manage to keep the sand off me long enough to get three degrees, earn several academic and orthodontic awards, and learn how to make teeth straight.

Following graduation from orthodontic residency, I went to work for Spillane Orthodontics—which became Spillane & Reynolds Orthodontics a few years later—and I still work there today. My wife grew up in Novi, so our family definitely feels at home. I added a few more jobs as well—consulting for various orthodontic companies as well as lecturing. To date, I have lectured in several countries on three continents. I have always been interested in treatments that are faster, more comfortable, and aesthetic, and I have participated in many, many clinical trials for products that help deliver patients what they are looking for: faster, clearer, better, and more affordable orthodontics.

Growing up in a blue-collar town in metro Detroit gave me great perspective on just how hard people work to earn a living, especially in my hometown. I have grown incredibly passionate about bringing world-class orthodontic treatment back home to the Detroit area, including opening an office in Rochester Hills, Michigan. Rochester Hills is the next town over from my hometown, Lake Orion, and it is also where I got my first job in the seventh grade, helping make apple cider at the Rochester Cider Mill. (Later, I waited tables at Olive Garden and at a Max & Erma's in downtown Birmingham.)

My journey to bring people world-class treatment is two pronged. First, I had to learn to become a world-class doctor and develop the clinical skills and knowledge necessary to bring innovative, leading-edge treatment to the locations around my practices. This led me around the world to attend meetings, visit orthodontic offices, and learn from the best and brightest orthodontists. As my skills developed, I was invited to participate in product development and clinical trials to help shape the future of the profession. I have now participated in many, many clinical trials, including some that have helped develop some of the most sophisticated clinical orthodontic technologies available today. This experience enabled me to begin teaching other orthodontists, and I have lectured around the world speaking on clinical excellence in orthodontics, high-tech orthodontics, and orthodontic practice management. Teaching has brought me in contact with an even wider variety of amazing doctors from around the world, which has and will continue to further my clinical education and experience in orthodontics.

The second aspect of my journey in orthodontics is to help make the best possible treatments affordable and available to as many people as I can. Every child deserves an amazing, healthy smile he or she can be proud of. Growing up in a blue-collar town outside of Detroit, I realized that orthodontics is a significant investment for many families. This understanding led me to cofound OrthoFi, a company that works with orthodontists and patients to help make high-quality, high-tech, leading-edge orthodontic treatment more affordable for more people. Giving people the faster, higher-quality, more comfortable treatment they want creates more expense for doctors, which causes them to feel significant financial pressure. This, in turn, can lead to high down payments as well as larger monthly payments for patients, which can make orthodontic treatment less affordable. OrthoFi is aimed at bridging the gaps between the high-tech treatments people want and the affordable payment options people need. It has been successful in helping tens of thousands of patients find affordable ways to start orthodontic treatment. I am excited for the future, helping make high-quality orthodontic treatment available for as many people and families as possible.

I also realize that even with very affordable financial terms, many families still cannot afford the orthodontic care they need. This led me to found the metro-Detroit chapter of the Smile for a Lifetime foundation, a charity aimed at providing smile scholarships for low-income families in desperate need of life-changing orthodontic services. Providing life-changing orthodontic treatment to those who could otherwise not afford it is very rewarding for both my team and me.

I hope that you will find this book to be informative, honest, and more than a little bit fun. (I know—teeth talk can be boring. Hopefully this isn't!) My goal is to help people and parents sort through the immense amount of confusing and, unfortunately, sometimes disingenuous information about straightening teeth and to help consumers make informed decisions. If this book helps you become a little smarter about orthodontics, it will have served its purpose.

You can find out more about me and our practice at www.MyAmazingSmile.com.

You can find out more about common orthodontic questions or ask me a question directly at www. AskDrReynolds.com.

Enjoy!

Jamie Reynolds, DDS, MS
Diplomate, American Board of Orthodontics

How to Choose Your Best Provider

You have brains in your head. You have feet in your shoes. You can steer yourself in any direction you choose. You're on your own, and you know what you know. And you are the guy who'll decide where to go.

—DR. SEUSS

Many people are confused about where to get their teeth straightened and why it matters which professional they choose. You have several choices:

1. An orthodontist
2. Your family dentist
3. A mail-order service
4. Yourself (gasp!)

Let's start with some definitions.

Orthodontist: Orthodontists are dentists who completed dental school and then attended a two- or three-year residency focused solely on orthodontics. Orthodontists focus their practice on improving tooth alignment, correcting bite problems, managing TMJ (temporomandibular joint) issues, and designing smiles. They limit their practices to orthodontics, so they do not do other dental services in their offices (such as fillings, cleanings, deep cleanings, root canals, tooth extractions, and so on). If someone offers braces (also called brackets) or Invisalign and also offers cleanings and fillings, he or she is *not* an orthodontist. An orthodontist is a specialist. A specialist in dentistry is similar to a specialist in medicine. You may be familiar with a variety of specialists in medicine, such as dermatologists, cardiologists, neurologists, plastic surgeons, and many more. In dentistry, specialists include orthodontists, periodontists (gum specialists), endodontists (root canal specialists), oral surgeons, and several others. Similar to those within medicine, dentistry's specialists are the most highly trained and highly skilled in their particular area of expertise.

Family dentist: The family dentist (also referred to as a general dentist, a cosmetic dentist, or a primary-care dentist) is an integral part of the dental system and is responsible for diagnosing and treating many of the key factors involved in a patient's dental health. The family dentist has completed dental school but has not completed a residency in specialty dentistry. Similar to your family medical doctor, your family dentist is responsible for ongoing evaluation of your overall dental care. Also similarly, your family dentist is responsible for diagnosing conditions for which seeking the opinion of a specialist is appropriate. Very little information on orthodontic treatment is given in dental school, as the focus is on diagnosing and treating other conditions. Significant training after dental school is necessary to deliver high-quality orthodontic treatment.

Let me be clear right now that the point of this chapter is *not* to imply that all orthodontic procedures should be completed only by orthodontists. I personally work with many family dentists who do a fine job of treating certain orthodontic cases and achieve very nice results. There is a spectrum of orthodontic cases, from simple all the way to very, very difficult. Where on the spectrum an individual case falls may determine by whom and where the case is best treated.

However, there is a worrisome trend in which a family dentist looking to add profit to the bottom line takes a weekend course in orthodontics and then misleads patients to believe that he or she can treat all or most orthodontic cases as effectively as a specialist can (often while taking his or her own family to a specialist for treatment). I cannot overemphasize this point enough: **a weekend course in any aspect of medicine or dentistry is not sufficient training to provide quality treatment of any medical or dental condition**. It takes years of training to be able to consistently treat orthodontic cases well. Whether they are orthodontic specialists or family dentists, those who consistently and continually—over the course of years, not days or weekends—pursue education and training to provide the highest possible level of orthodontic care are the professionals you want to place your trust in.

So how do you choose a doctor for your family's orthodontic treatment? I have composed a series of questions you can ask to help you choose a doctor who has a high chance of providing quality care for you and your family. These questions will also help you identify the unscrupulous doctor who may be trying to deceive you as to his or her orthodontic experience in order to profit from providing services.

Here are the questions.

1. *Are you an orthodontist?* The answer to this question should be a simple yes or no. If the answer is longer than that, the person is likely trying to think of ways to convince you that being an orthodontist doesn't matter. This is a good clue that the doctor is not qualified or experienced enough to give quality care. However, below are some follow-up questions. A good, genuine family dentist who does orthodontics well will answer these questions honestly and be forthright about his or her training and experience. Again, if you detect any hesitation or deflection

in the answers, consider it a clear sign that you should seek a second opinion from a specialist before starting orthodontic treatment.

2. *Did you go to a full-time, accredited residency, or did you take a course?* Again, you should get a simple answer. Remember, weekend courses are not sufficient to confer a high level of experience or skill. Also, the term *full time* is key. Why? Many people are now advertising that they've attended a two-year residency when the education was in fact only a few courses taken over a two-year time span. *Be careful (in any aspect of life) with those who appear to be misleading or deceptive.* The goal here is to determine the training level of your future orthodontic provider—nothing more, nothing less. More training is better. If the doctor did not attend a full-time residency, you may want to consider the opinion of a specialist.

If you do decide to further consider a doctor who did not attend a full-time residency, what do you ask next?

3. *If you took a course, was it a weekend course or a longer one?* Find out how often the course met and for how long. Again, the goal here is to determine the training and skill level of the provider. A longer course taught over several sessions extending over several years is better than a course taught in a day or several days.

4. Will the treatment you recommend correct my bite? Many patients, and unfortunately many dental providers, really do not have a concept of how important your bite is to your overall dental health. If you have crooked teeth, you likely also have a bite problem, and you will benefit greatly from having any bite problems corrected. If anyone tells you that many people have bite problems and they do just fine, you may want to consider another opinion (see Chapter 3: Why Should I Care about My Bite?).

5. How many cases like mine have you treated? Most doctors who have treated many cases will keep books of before-and-after photos. Ask to see photos of cases similar to yours. Evaluate whether you like the way the results look.

6. Have you or any of your family members been treated by an orthodontist? With those who answer yes, you may want to consider why they would take *their* family to an orthodontist but are recommending they treat *your* family.

7. Have you ever treated someone with aligners or braces that went wrong and you had to ask an orthodontist for help? A yes to this question may not be a poor answer. Beginning an orthodontic case that is more difficult than it first seemed, recognizing the challenges that lie ahead, and then seeking the help of a more experienced provider speaks more of honesty and integrity than it does of lack of expertise.

Asking these seven simple questions will help you gain insight into the level of skill, expertise, and professionalism of the doctor in whom you or a loved one may place your trust.

Mail-order orthodontics: Mail-order service is a new trend in all areas of health care. In some cases, it makes sense. Consider products such as mail-order contact lenses, for example: an eye doctor fits them for you, and then you replace the lenses as you wear them out. Regardless of where you buy them, the contacts are the same, so ordering online when you need more makes sense. You will also know if you are no longer seeing well, which will prompt you to visit an eye doctor for your next exam.

However, moving your teeth is a complicated process. First, and most important, you need clearance from your family dentist *before* you begin to move teeth. We see many patients who haven't seen a dentist in many years, so the first thing we recommend is a cleaning and checkup at a dentist. If you have active gum disease, you can cause more harm than good if you try to move teeth. Most mail-order options don't care if you have had a cleaning or if you have cavities. Why? Probably because the companies are run by businesspeople, not doctors who have sworn an oath to "do no harm." Big business often cares more about money than it cares about you. Consider this fact before taking your local doctor out of the loop.

Second, dental appliances are not like contact lenses. Each at-home aligner you use creates tooth movement. One thing all aligner treatments have in common is that the teeth don't always move as planned. For this reason, using aligners for unsupervised tooth movement can lead to teeth moving in undesired ways.

Third, if something happens during the manufacturing process or while you wear the aligners and the aligners are damaged or broken, wearing them can lead to serious problems with your bite that can cause long-term damage to your teeth or gums. You don't want that. So please have your treatment supervised by a professional so that you get the outcome you want and have paid for: beautifully straight teeth and a healthy bite.

Do-it-yourself (DIY) treatment: A new (and unfortunate) fad in health care, DIY treatment strikes fear into the heart of any health-care provider, and this is not because we are worrying about losing market share. We have all seen crazy things happen to people who try at-home remedies for their health problems.

I have one question for all the DIY orthodontists out there: *Really*? I know some may think you just stick the braces on and then the teeth move by homing beacon to the exact perfect spot, every time. In reality, it is very difficult to move teeth into a position that is both nice to look at and doesn't cause tooth problems or headaches. If you don't believe me, humor me a little: get on the Internet and search Google for "DIY braces fail." Don't just take it from me. See what can happen when you do it yourself. Ouch! Use what you find as mental ammunition to avoid DIY fillings, heart catheterizations, brain surgeries, or any other health procedure that has a DIY craze. Do-it-yourselfing is great for stuff around the house (although I personally avoid anything that involves electrical work). But just because you can find metal and wire at Home Depot does not mean that DIY braces are a good idea. I strongly recommend you reconsider if you are remotely thinking of a do-it-yourself treatment.

When looking for an orthodontic provider, keep in mind that the best possible scenario (other than being lucky to have naturally perfect teeth) is to correct your bite early. Many times, people with what appear to be very straight teeth need orthodontics more than people with minor or moderately crooked teeth, because their bite is off. This circumstance is often difficult for parents to understand, as differences in bite can seem subtle to anyone other than a trained professional.

In today's world, it is absolutely warranted to be skeptical of anyone and everything, including doctors.

I get it. I am often skeptical of health advice for my own kids and family. **When in doubt, get a second opinion.** If you get a few opinions that are consistent, chances are that the treatment is in your best interest. And, when I say second opinion, I do not count Google, blogs, or your friend's cousin's uncle who had braces once. I mean that you should visit several orthodontic specialists. Google, friends, and blogs are great places to start when researching which specialist to visit first. However, there is a lot of misinformation about *all* health care—including orthodontics—on the Internet. Remember: most people don't even know how many teeth you are supposed to have in your mouth (answer: thirty-two, including wisdom teeth). If you had a problem with your finger, would you accept medical advice about hand treatments from someone who didn't know how many fingers you are supposed to have? Of course you wouldn't. So it probably doesn't make sense to trust the blogs that opine on the viability and quality of different orthodontic treatments. Find an orthodontist. If you don't like the first one or feel a hint of skepticism, find another one that your intuition tells you to trust. Then let the orthodontist do his or her thing.

Also, before choosing a provider, it is necessary to look in the mirror and have a realistic conversation with yourself. Here is a quick analogy that may help. Imagine that you wanted to change your hair color from brown to blond. The cheapest possible way is to buy some peroxide and have at it. This works for some people. However, if you are looking for a cut, color, and style that Jennifer Aniston or David Beckham would be proud of, well, you need something entirely different. For your smile, is cost the most important factor? If so, is it OK to take the peroxide approach? Improved results cost more. It takes expensive products and skill to get better results. You cannot get a Jennifer Aniston result in your bathroom from a bottle of peroxide. Nor can you get a beautiful smile from cheap braces and unskilled doctors or do-it-yourself options.

When shopping for an orthodontist, many people think they are all exactly alike, but they're not. The analogy I use to illustrate this point is shopping for golf clubs. If you went to several stores to look for a new driver, it would be natural to consider the one that was on sale or lower in price. Any club can consistently and reliably put the golf ball where it is supposed to go. However, the same club can also direct the ball repeatedly into the bushes or the pond. *The results you get from your new club will vary substantially according to who swings it.* Golf clubs are commodities. Big Bertha drivers are all made the same. Hence, it can make sense to shop purely on price. Doctors are *not* commodities. They are not all alike. With a doctor, you are buying the swing, not the club, even if the doctor is using the same treatment type, like braces or Invisalign. There are different levels of skill, commitment, and expertise involved.

Choosing based on price alone may not always be the wisest decision when it comes to your health care. You likely would not choose the buy-one-get-one-free heart surgeon or the cheapest brain surgeon in town. Make sure your results are going where you want them to and not into the bushes. Remember, all doctors are *not* created alike. There is skill, art, training, and expertise involved in each patient's care. Be sure you do your homework and know exactly what you are buying when it comes to your family's health care.

So what's the moral of this story? To begin with, avoid do-it-yourself health care like the plague. There is a reason it takes so long to become a doctor. And it's not because we are greedy or have nothing better to do. The reason is that a lot of factors must be considered in any health-care procedure, and nothing is as easy as it looks. Don't do it yourself with health care. If you must be a hard-core DIYer, think bathroom remodeling or a new fireplace—or publishing a book (like me). Not braces!

Second, do your research when it comes to orthodontic treatment. Not all doctors are created equal. Remember to ask tough questions if you are not going to see a specialist for your orthodontic care. But don't be afraid to ask the orthodontist tough questions as well. There are, unfortunately, many orthodontists who have not kept up with current improvements in treatment and technology.

Use your gut feeling, and if anything doesn't seem right to you, get a second opinion. Since most orthodontic exams are free, all you invest in a second opinion is your time. Your smile and your dental health are investments you make in yourself and in your or your loved one's future. The time, energy, and dollars you are investing in a new smile and a healthy bite should last a lifetime!

Why Should I Care about My Bite?

Learn from yesterday, live for today, hope for tomorrow. The important thing is not to stop questioning.

—Albert Einstein

Why *should* you care about your bite? This is actually a much more complicated question than it sounds. The way teeth fit together is, believe it or not, very complicated. Anyone who has had a new filling or crown off by a bit (we typically say the filling is "high") knows that having your bite off can be a real pain—literally. There are five main problems that can occur when your bite is off: tooth pain, temporomandibular joint (TMJ) pain, jaw muscle (this also can be labeled TMJ) pain, tooth wear, and gum recession.

There are some people whose bite doesn't fit together well (also known as having a "bad bite"), yet they have very few, if any, of the foregoing symptoms. There are also people who drink like a fish and smoke like a chimney but live to be a hundred years old. They are few, but they do exist. Most who smoke or drink in excess realize sooner rather than later that there are health consequences to their behavior. Similarly, when their bite is off, many people eventually make their way to a dentist or orthodontist or periodontist (or all of the above) to deal with the consequences. Here is the lowdown on the long-term consequences of your bite being off:

1. **Tooth pain**. A bite that is off by a fraction of a millimeter can cause tooth pain. Improperly adjusted dental work can irritate a nerve. Tooth pain from these factors usually happens quickly and is usually the result of trauma or dental work. Move a tooth a fraction out of alignment and it can hurt. This happens, by the way, in even the most skilled orthodontist's hands. Sometimes, to move a tooth from point A to point B requires it to be in the "wrong" spot temporarily on its journey to the right one. It is important to have the eventual position of the tooth correct to prevent long-term issues (see numbers 4 and 5 below).

2. **Jaw joint (TMJ) pain**. Your jaw joint is made up of two bony parts: the temporal bone in your skull and your lower jaw (the mandible). Put the temporal bone and the mandible together, and you get the temporomandibular joint (TMJ). Between the temporal bone and the mandible is a cushion called a disc. Similar to other joints, this disc keeps the bones from grinding on each other. Occasionally,

trauma to the joint can result in a wrinkle in the disc that can create a crackling or popping sound when you open or close your jaw. For most people, popping in the jaw joint is no big deal and can be considered normal. In fact, most jaw joint noises are normal. When I was a teenager, my mother's knees would make a cracking sound when-ever she bent down to pick something up off the floor (un-doubtedly from a mess I had created and failed to clean up—my mother was a saint). This was a normal sound for her knees. No surgery or treatment was necessary, and there was no pain. Jaw joints can behave similarly.

However, if you have a hard time opening your jaw, can't open it at all, or have significant pain during jaw movement, you should be evaluated for TMJ problems. Significant problems with your jaw joint are broadly called temporomandibular disorder, or TMD. TMD can be a re-sult of jaw joint pain, issues with opening and closing, or muscular pain (or a combination of the three).

A quick note here: surgeries on the TMJ are notorious-ly unsuccessful. For reasons we have yet to understand, jaw joint surgeries are nowhere near as successful as sur-geries on other joints, like knees and hips. It is very com-mon for knee surgery to be successful and for the patient to benefit long term from the procedure. However, it is very rare for a patient to have long-term positive benefits from TMJ surgery. If you are considering surgery, be sure you have exhausted all other options. Only proceed if several opinions say that surgery is your only option and your last resort.

3. **Muscular pain**. Muscular pain is the most common finding in people with TMD and is largely responsible for the pain associated with many headaches. If you are having unexplainable headaches, you should see an orthodontist to have your bite evaluated. Believe it or not, many headache varieties—including migraine headaches—can be caused by bite issues. I have personally eliminated headaches for many people who have "tried everything" with no success. When evaluating muscular-generated headaches, it is critical to have an intricate knowledge of the anatomy and function of the muscles of the jaw and face. Orthodontists are exquisitely trained in the area of the head and neck. They also understand the intricacies of the bite and should be able to determine if the bite and muscular pain are related and can be relieved with changes to the bite.

Headaches are an incredibly complex topic, and many books have been devoted to the subject. Suffice it to say that if you are having headaches you don't know the source of, you should see a specialist. If you have seen many traditional medical doctors (family physician, neurologist, and so on) for the problem without success, have an orthodontist evaluate your bite to see if your headaches could be related.

4. **Tooth wear.** Your teeth function as a chewing machine. And, just as with any other machine, the parts need to fit together properly to prevent premature wear. Teeth that do not fit properly can grind like gears in a wheel that do not mesh together appropriately. Over time, teeth can wear so that the inside part of the tooth becomes exposed. The outside of the tooth is called enamel, and the inside is called dentin. As soon as the dentin, which is much softer than enamel, becomes exposed, it will wear much more quickly and will become significantly discolored. When dentin is exposed, fillings are typically not enough to fix the problem, and crowns become necessary.

Once tooth wear progresses to a certain point, significant dental work *and* orthodontics are necessary to correct the problem. Thus preventing significant tooth wear *before* it happens is the best approach.

5. **Gum wear.** As my practice is outside Detroit, I use a lot of car analogies in explaining things to my patients. Your teeth being off slightly is similar to the tires on your car being slightly out of alignment. You can still drive a car whose wheels are out of alignment; however, you may experience significant shaking at certain speeds. If your car shakes at seventy miles an hour, you can still drive it,

but the shaking will eventually cause issues not only with the tires but also in other parts of the car. Your teeth are no different. Not only will the teeth prematurely wear, but the gums and supporting bone will also prematurely wear. Notching of the teeth near the gumline (called *abfraction*) and wearing away of the gum tissue (called *gingival recession*) are very common in people over thirty whose bite is off. Gum recession and tooth notching can be very painful as well as difficult and expensive to fix.

Again, prevention by correcting your bite early is the best option. I see people in the office weekly who say, "Everything was great until recently. My teeth are getting crooked, and my bite is changing." Your bite is something that can be off for a while and not cause you a lot of problems—until it does. Some people's bites catch up with them in their twenties and some in their sixties—or at any age in between. All I can tell you, after seeing tens of thousands of patients, is that eventually your bite *will* catch up with you. Dealing with bite issues proactively is much less painful, less labor intensive, and less expensive than dealing with bite problems later. Problems with your bite can literally come back to bite you.

Does My Seven-Year-Old Really Need Braces?

The secret of getting ahead is getting started.

—Mark Twain

One of the questions I field all the time is, "When is the right time to start treatment?" This is a confusing topic. Depending on whom you ask, you will get a variety of answers about what treatment is necessary and when and how exactly it should proceed. Getting more opinions doesn't always help, as there are many different orthodontic gadgets and gizmos that different doctors use to correct the same problem. Confusing! You may end up with several different—and even conflicting—opinions. So I will give my two cents on the age of treatment. I hope to provide some clarity rather than add to the confusion.

For growing children—especially those who don't have all their permanent teeth yet—the best timing for treatment can vary. Let me be clearer: different kiddos can have different problems, and each type of problem has different treatments, each of which has a different ideal timing.

The American Association of Orthodontists recommends that all children see an orthodontist by age seven. This may seem shockingly early. I often field questions from people who believe that the only reason orthodontists want to see patients that early is to pad their own pockets. It is true that any profession—from car repair to gardening to health care and more—has members who unscrupulously recommend unnecessary procedures solely for personal profit. However, most people are just trying to do the right thing—and orthodontists are no different. They make the most money not by treating any particular person but by treating many, many people—the only way a practice truly grows and thrives is by doing right by its clientele and gaining people's trust (and thereby referrals). This comes from service providers treating everyone as they would their own families.

The orthodontist examines children at age seven or eight to screen for problems that need early intervention (about 20 percent of cases). Most kids can wait for treatment until they are twelve or thirteen, when it can be done in a single phase (called comprehensive treatment). For those with problems calling for earlier help, the typical recommendation is for two-phase treatment, with the later portion delayed until the child is a bit older.

The reason that you want to consider bringing your child in to the orthodontist between ages seven and eight is that certain conditions are treated better when the patient is younger. There are four major things the orthodontist looks for at this point:

1. *Are the jaws growing properly?* The growth of the jaws and face is a very complicated subject that takes years of graduate school to understand. We will not be covering this topic fully here. However, it is important to know a few things about jaw growth and development. First, the upper jaw stops growing around age eight, which is much earlier than the lower jaw (or the rest of the body) stops growing. Because of this, orthodontists can identify issues with the growth of the upper jaw earlier and can recommend treatment of upper-jaw growth deficiencies. The upper jaw is "stretchier" at a younger age, and expansion of the jaw is much easier and much more stable before age ten.

The following is a brief list (orthodontists like gizmos, and there are too many to list them all here) of common jaw-growth appliances and their basic functions:

Upper expander. The most common growth issue is that the upper jaw is not wide enough. Deficiency here has a variety of possible causes, including prolonged thumb or finger habits, airway issues such as enlarged tonsils or adenoids, mouth breathing, allergies, or genetics. You may hear the word *crossbite*, which describes a condition that is usually the result of a narrow or underdeveloped upper jaw. Typically, issues with upper-jaw width are treated with a rapid palatal expander, or RPE. This device works because the upper jaw is actually two halves—right and left—separated by a growth plate. The expander stretches the growth plate, which permanently widens the upper jaw.

Lower expander. Some orthodontists recommend a lower expander to help with crowding of the lower teeth. This is effective at creating room but is a bit of a misnomer, as the lower jaw is made up of only one bone. An expander only tips teeth wider; it does not actually cause the lower jaw to grow wider. Also, lower expanders are quite a mouthful and interfere with speech and chewing. Think hockey puck. So while lower expanders can work, I rarely, if ever, recommend them, as braces widen the lower area equally effectively and are much easier on the patient.

Headgear. Ah, the dreaded headgear—the bane of many a person born in the sixties and seventies. Headgear is an appliance designed to correct overbite (buck teeth) by pulling the upper teeth and jaw back, and it can be very effective. However, most overbites are .not caused by the upper jaw being too far forward but by the lower jaw being too far back. So even though headgear can still be effective in correcting an overbite, it is rarely the right choice, as developing the lower jaw is more important than restricting the growth of the upper jaw. Plus, headgear looks like an eighteenth-century torture device, and today's teen is not likely to wear it, no matter how effective it may be. Anyone recommending headgear may be behind the times, as there are newer advances in orthodontic treatment and technology—and that's a reason to get a second opinion. I have not used headgear to treat an overbite since completing my residency in 2002. There are better ways.

Face mask. The protraction face mask is designed to do the opposite of headgear (it is often called "reverse headgear") and is aimed at correcting underbites by helping the upper jaw grow forward. Face masks should not be confused with regular headgear. Face-mask treatment is also very effective and can often help patients avoid future surgical procedures. In fact, my oldest son was successfully treated with a face mask, and it dramatically improved the growth of his upper jaw. The best time to use a face mask is before age ten; effectiveness of treatment falls off significantly after that because the upper jaw stops growing early. Also, face-mask treatment is almost always combined with an upper expander (as was the case for my son).

Functional appliance. The functional appliance is a newer appliance designed to replace traditional headgear. Its goal is to encourage growth of the lower jaw to correct overbites. Deficient lower-jaw growth is the underlying reason in almost all cases of medium or large overbite. Functional appliances come in an almost limitless number of shapes, sizes, and names. It seems that every orthodontist in the eighties and nineties tried to get one of these gizmos named after him or her. Here is a quick list of the more popular functional appliances: Herbst, MARA, Bionator, Frankel, Twin Block, Jasper Jumper, Forsus, BioBite Corrector, Bite Fixer, PowerScope, and Activator. There are many others.

Functional appliances are of two main types: removable and fixed. Removable appliances are removed for cleaning, eating, and the like. Fixed appliances are secured in the mouth and not removed until treatment ends. Personally, I prefer the fixed variety. Why? Because I know that some people are not compliant in wearing appliances. The removable ones therefore automatically lower the success rate of treatment. I like to get the best outcomes as often as possible, and I find that appliances that the patient cannot remove dramatically increase the quality of the results. Plus, new designs in Herbst and MARA appliances mean they are smaller than ever, and patients can adapt to them very quickly. Also, advances in types that attach directly to the braces (currently Forsus, BioBite Corrector, and PowerScope) also make wearing these appliances easy and effective, and their placement and removal are easy on both doctor and patient.

2. *Is there enough room for the teeth to grow in*? Another major reason to consider two-phase treatment is if the teeth do not have enough room to grow in properly. When a tooth cannot grow in because there is something in the way (usually another tooth or an extra tooth) or because it is growing in the wrong direction (usually because there is something in the way), that tooth is said to be impacted.

Impacted teeth are a big pain to deal with for both doctor and patient. Mechanically, it is much harder for the doctor to get access to impacted teeth and reliably and predictably bring them into the proper position. Impacted teeth can often lead to less-than-ideal results.

For the patient, this scenario often requires a small surgery to uncover the tooth so that the orthodontist can begin to straighten it. This surgery increases the pain and discomfort associated with the treatment as well as the cost. Additional surgical procedures (often requiring an oral surgeon) add to the time and technique needed to straighten these teeth. Early intervention can often create enough room for teeth to grow in properly, thus making future treatment much easier and more comfortable for the patient. Many, many impactions can be avoided by early interceptive (phase-one) treatment.

There are several ways to create more room for teeth to grow in. These include the use of many of the appliances mentioned above that help improve jaw growth and jaw structure. Braces may also be used to create space for teeth to grow in.

The other option is removal of teeth. Removal of teeth falls into two categories, discussed below.

Removal of baby teeth. The removal of baby teeth is a common way to help the permanent teeth grow in. The natural course for losing a baby tooth starts when the permanent tooth growing under it puts pressure on its roots, causing the root to start dissolving. When the root gets short enough, the baby tooth falls out, and the new tooth grows in. Occasionally, however, the baby tooth root does not dissolve the way it should. It then becomes a roadblock and causes the permanent tooth to grow in a funny direction, often leading to impaction of the permanent tooth. Removal of a baby tooth whose root isn't dissolving as it should can allow the permanent tooth to grow in normally and prevent the costly and painful extra procedures necessary to deal with impacted teeth. No one wants to have teeth pulled. However, removing a misbehaving baby tooth is oftentimes the simplest and best solution to a problem that could become much bigger.

Removal of permanent teeth. Another way to create space for a permanent tooth to grow in is to remove another permanent tooth. For many doctors, myself included, removal of permanent teeth has become more of a last resort than a treatment of choice. In days gone by, up to 75 percent of cases treated in an orthodontic practice included removal of permanent teeth. Today, early intervention and dramatic improvements in braces technologies have drastically reduced the number of patients who are best treated with permanent-tooth extraction. In my practice, less than 1 percent of all patients undergo removal of permanent teeth.

If an orthodontist you consult recommends permanent-tooth extraction, I strongly suggest that you consider getting a second opinion. This is not to say that removal of permanent teeth is never necessary or is grounds for malpractice. However, some doctors have not kept up to speed with today's advanced treatments and may be recommending extractions when modern orthodontic techniques could treat equally or better, without removals. Getting multiple opinions when permanent-tooth extraction is recommended is prudent. Once the teeth are removed, they are gone for good.

3. *How are the teeth that are not yet in the mouth developing—and are the correct number of teeth present?* The final major criterion evaluated at orthodontic exams is the presence or absence of the correct number of permanent teeth. An orthodontist uses a panoramic x-ray or a 3-D cone-beam computed tomography scan (CBCT), which provide a wider field of view than the x-rays typically used by general dentists. Because of this, missing or extra teeth are often diagnosed for the first time in the orthodontist's office.

Before I went to dental school, I assumed that everyone had the same number of teeth (like with fingers and toes). Although some people are born with a different number of fingers or toes (I have a cousin who was born with an extra pinky toe), this condition is pretty rare. In an orthodontic office, however, it is not unusual to see many people who have missing or extra teeth. In fact, I see several patients a day with missing teeth—most of whom assume that this is very unusual.

The following is some information to consider about missing or extra teeth.

Extra teeth. The presence of extra teeth typically causes more orthodontic problems than missing teeth. Extra teeth cause the other teeth to develop out of place and often lead to crowding, rotations, and impacted teeth. Extra teeth can appear anywhere in the mouth, although the most common place is between the two upper front teeth. An extra tooth is called a *supernumerary tooth*, and one between the upper two front teeth is called a *mesiodens*. A mesiodens has its own special name because it is the most common type.

Because extra teeth can cause lots of unwanted trouble, early screening is key. More often than not, supernumerary teeth never become normal-looking or normal-functioning teeth, so they are often removed. Also, many times two-phase treatment is necessary to undo the issues caused by extra teeth.

Missing teeth. Missing teeth are more common than extra teeth. While it is very important to identify that teeth are missing, treatment is typically not initiated until all other permanent teeth have grown in. Unlike extra teeth, which create crowding and developmental issues, missing teeth typically do not cause problems with development. Sometimes they are preceded by a missing baby tooth, but it is very common to have the correct number of baby teeth yet be missing one or more permanent teeth. The correct number of teeth for an adult is thirty-two. The record number of missing teeth I have seen in my office is fourteen, although it is much more common to be missing one to three teeth. We see several patients per day who are missing teeth. These patients need special considerations and skilled planning to yield excellent orthodontic results.

Teeth can be missing anywhere in the mouth, but the more common places for this include the lower second-premolar area (just before the molars) and the upper lateral-incisor area (the teeth next to the two front teeth). Many times, when a permanent tooth doesn't grow in, the baby tooth just stays in its place for many years. It is not uncommon for me to see baby teeth last into someone's thirties and forties. Sometimes, though, they loosen and fall out before the teenage years. Also, sometimes a developmental problem with the baby tooth requires it to be extracted, even though the permanent tooth underneath is missing. The management of missing teeth is a difficult and complicated topic that is beyond the scope of this book. However, early identification and management will help with developing an appropriate treatment plan to achieve the best result for the patient.

4. *Does the child snore, and is there an airway obstruction?* The medical profession is paying more and more attention to something called sleep apnea. Sleep apnea is a condition in which a person will temporarily stop breathing while he or she is sleeping. Repetitive bouts of not breathing, called episodes, can cause serious health problems. Sleep apnea that is left untreated over time is now believed to be a significant factor in premature death as well as many other health issues.

We are now realizing that sleep apnea can start at a very early age. Patients can be diagnosed with pediatric sleep apnea as early as four or five years old. Pediatric sleep apnea can lead to deficiencies in mental and physical development including ADHD and learning impairments as well as a decrease in physical development and constant daytime sleepiness. The body needs oxygen to grow and develop and repeated untreated episodes of sleep apnea can interfere with normal growth and development.

There are several types of sleep apnea, the most common and most treatable being obstructive sleep apnea, or OSA. A very common symptom of OSA is snoring. When most of us think of snoring, we think of grandpa asleep on the La-Z-Boy, making a hacking chainsaw noise. In children, snoring sounds more like a kitten purring than a chainsaw.

If you notice snoring (or purring, in a child) with repeated bouts during which it appears the person is holding his or her breath, seek an evaluation for obstructive sleep apnea. An expander can be a very effective, and sometimes life-changing, treatment for obstructive sleep apnea.

As most orthodontists offer complimentary exams, it is a good idea to have your kiddo checked out by an orthodontist at age seven. If no treatment is indicated, then a good and ethical doctor will not recommend any. However, if treatment is indicated, then dividing it into two phases can yield exponentially better and more predictable results. Call your local orthodontist today to set up a screening for your seven-year-old to keep little problems from snowballing into big problems.

Think Twice before Having Permanent Teeth Removed

It is not the strongest of the species that survive, nor the most intelligent, but the one most responsive to change.

—Charles Darwin

Orthodontics has changed dramatically in the past twenty years. Throughout the seventies and eighties, most orthodontic cases, for a variety of reasons, required the extraction of permanent teeth. Unfortunately, extracting teeth can result in long-term detrimental effects on many patients' facial structures and compromise the health of their gums and bones.

One of the common questions that patients ask when seeking orthodontic care is whether they need to have teeth extracted. Nobody wants to go through having teeth pulled if it can be avoided. A full complement of teeth often results in a fuller, more beautiful smile.

So what has changed to allow orthodontists to avoid the extraction of so many teeth? The answers are provided below.

The test of time. As more and more people were treated with braces over the years, orthodontists were able to see what happened to these patients as they became adults and aged. What they saw was not encouraging. Orthodontists realized that as people age, their lips tend to flatten out naturally. In patients who had permanent teeth extracted, this flattening was magnified significantly due to reduced support for the lips. As orthodontists began seeing this negative aging process caused by extractions, they began seeking other ways to treat.

Controlled research. In the eighties, the University of Michigan began researching what caused people to have crowded teeth. Many times, orthodontists told people that their teeth were just too big to fit. Were people's teeth too big? Interestingly enough, research has shown that this was not the case at all. In fact, virtually everyone had the same sizes of teeth, but those who had crowding had much smaller dental arches than those who had no crowding. The conclusion was that orthodontic treatment options should focus more on creating additional room for crowded teeth instead of removing teeth.

Bonds instead of bands. Do you remember those rings around teeth with braces? Until the late seventies, these rings, called bands, were the only way to connect braces to the teeth. Then a process called bonding came along. Bonding uses a thin layer of adhesive to connect a brace to the front surface of a tooth. Bands around each tooth added about five millimeters of material between the teeth. Because of this, even in mildly crowded cases, there just was not enough room to fit all the teeth in the mouth.

Better wires. Materials that NASA has tested in space are now incorporated into the wires used in orthodontics. These wires deliver a force on the teeth that is much lighter and gentler on the teeth than that of the stainless steel wires used with traditional braces. Due to this gentleness, teeth are now able to move in a way that allows the bone to adapt and change with the movement, and orthodontists are able to treat more cases without tooth extractions.

Better braces. The final piece to the puzzle arrived on the scene in the new millennium. Braces traditionally have required something to hold the wire in place (also referred to as "tightening" the braces). This was done with either small wire ties or those fun little colored elastics. Although these ties kept the wires in place, they caused friction and kept the teeth from sliding freely. Around the year 2000, a new type of brace was invented that does not require ties to hold the wire in place. Instead, a door or clip opens and closes to hold the wire in place. There is no friction against the wire, so the teeth are free to slide, and the orthodontist does not need to push as hard to get the teeth to move (which means less pain!).

Remember those space-age wires I mentioned? Now they can be made to push even more gently, and the bone adapts to make room for the teeth without extractions or expanders. This technique makes more space for the teeth just as the University of Michigan recommended. The perfect formula is finally available to orthodontists.

Having permanent teeth extracted is not a pleasant experience, and patients seek ways to avoid it. Long-term results have shown that permanent-tooth extractions can result in unwanted aging changes if performed on the wrong patient. Research proved that people's teeth are generally not too big, and the current recommendation is to make more room to accommodate the teeth rather than remove them. The perfect combination of technology has arrived, allowing orthodontists to accomplish the desired nonextraction treatment.

Extractions are no longer needed in over 99 percent of orthodontic patients. As a prospective patient,

you need to advocate for yourself in your own treatment. If you are recommended to have permanent teeth extracted, be sure to get a second opinion.

How to Get a Beautiful Smile without Being a "Metal Mouth"

There are only two mistakes one can make along the road to truth; not going all the way, and not starting.

—BUDDHA

In today's ever-changing world, the emphasis on aesthetics and beauty is greater than ever. Many factors have made having a beautiful smile more desirable and accessible today: reality TV, makeover shows, tooth-whitening products, social media, countless celebrities with ultra-white smiles, and more. A beautiful smile is probably the most important nonverbal aspect of a first impression. It's been said that Oprah stated on her show that she assumes people with crooked teeth are poor or not intelligent. More and more adults are seeking orthodontic treatment to help create the smiles they have always dreamed of.

Fortunately, we are keeping our teeth for life these days, but that wasn't always the case. Remember, until relatively recently, most people would have lost their teeth to decay by their thirties or forties—remember Grandma's dentures? However, if your bite is off, you may eventually have trouble with cracked teeth, tooth wear, gum recession, and notching of the teeth by the gumline, or abfraction. Not only is it important that your smile look great, but the way your bite comes together needs to be healthy as well. So with so many adults now seeking orthodontic treatment, the question often is, "Do I have to be a 'metal mouth'?" The answer is no—you also have cosmetic, or clear, options. Each has its own set of pros and cons.

Invisalign. Of all the clear options to move teeth, Invisalign is the most aesthetic. Over the past decade, through great marketing and word of mouth, Invisalign has become a household name. And why wouldn't it be? Orthodontic treatment without braces? Yes, please!

Invisalign is a series of clear, retainer-like trays called aligners. Aligners are typically worn one to two weeks at a time before the patient switches to a new aligner that is slightly different. After a series of these aligners, the teeth gradually become straight. One caution before choosing Invisalign: have a serious conversation with yourself and make sure you possess the self-discipline necessary to wear the aligners throughout treatment. Many treatments are completed in under a year, but more difficult cases can take two years or more, and that requires discipline to continue wearing the aligners. If you don't think you can do this, you should strongly consider clear braces or lingual braces (see below).

Invisalign can be done by any licensed dentist. However, many dentists learn to do Invisalign over a weekend course only and may not be best equipped to treat or even identify more complicated treatment. The great advantage of having Invisalign treatment performed by an orthodontist rather than a family dentist is that orthodontists can combine treatment methods with the aligners in tricky cases and get some really great results. The other advantage of being treated by an orthodontist is that if things just aren't progressing as planned, he or she can always fall back on braces if necessary. Prospective patients tell me all the time that they heard Invisalign doesn't work, which couldn't be further from the truth. It is important to know who is using the procedure before you judge whether it works or not—just like that new golf club. Being in the hands of an experienced specialist is comforting, to be sure.

Pros

- It is the most aesthetic option for moving teeth.
- Aligners can be removed for eating.
- It makes keeping teeth clean easy.

Cons

- It cannot be used to treat difficult cases.
- Discipline is required to wear the trays all day and night for many months.
- It is often offered by dentists with very limited training, which may lead to less-than-ideal results.

Clear braces. Although Invisalign is the most aesthetic option, it has its limitations. On a scale of one to ten, Invisalign tops out with cases that are a five or six in difficulty, even under the care of the most skilled orthodontist. In more challenging cases, the best option may be clear braces. There are many types of these. My favorite is currently the Damon Clear system. All other clear braces require clear elastic bands to hold the wire and brace together, and this band can discolor from strong-colored food and drink (spaghetti, coffee, wine) and collect bacteria. The Damon Clear system does not require bands (little doors built into the brace keep the wire secure), so the braces stay very clear—fairly translucent—throughout treatment. These braces are not noticeable when you are more than only a few feet away.

Pros

- The system can treat more difficult problems.
- Braces are much clearer than they used to be.
- Braces are virtually unnoticeable in photos.

Cons

- Braces are slightly less aesthetic than Invisalign.
- Braces are prone to the same problems that conventional braces have, such as poking wires and breakage.

Lingual braces. Lingual braces go on the inside of your teeth. They *do* work; however, they are technically challenging for even the most gifted orthodontist, so it may be difficult to find a practitioner who offers them (and they are also much more expensive than traditional braces or Invisalign). While braces on the inside of your teeth might have the advantage of great aesthetics, most patients agree that the disadvantages of slurred speech and sores on the tongue far outweigh their good looks. With the advent of Invisalign, the use of lingual braces has significantly decreased. However, some businesspeople and celebrities still choose lingual braces to improve their smiles.

Pros

- They are more aesthetic than clear braces.
- They can be an alternative to Invisalign for more difficult cases.

Cons

- They make speaking more difficult.
- They are not comfortable.

- They are more expensive than other options.
- Treatment can take longer, with more visits.

Instant orthodontics. Instant orthodontics has been popularized because of its catchy name and its visibility on reality makeover shows. However, instant orthodontics is not really orthodontics at all. It is a restorative dental procedure involving a combination of porcelain crowns, root canals, and tooth extraction to give the teeth a straight appearance. Instead of orthodontic tooth movement, teeth are ground down and replaced by porcelain caps or porcelain bridges. This approach is typically not the best option unless you have worn-down, severely decayed, or discolored teeth.

It's been said that producer Jerry Bruckheimer told Ben Affleck that to be cast in the lead of the movie *Armageddon*, he would need a movie-star smile. A quick Google search can verify that Ben had some serious work done to his teeth around that time. Because Ben's bite had caused significant wear to his teeth and he didn't have months to wait for traditional orthodontics, instant orthodontics made sense. If you have the lead in an upcoming multi-million-dollar movie, instant orthodontics may be for you.

A significant negative aspect of excessive restorative work in the place of orthodontics is that porcelain dental work needs replacement every so often. Crowns, bridges, and veneers have an average lifespan of only seven to ten years. In ideal situations, these restorations last twenty or more years. So unless you are older, the odds of needing to replace all the work later are pretty high. Instant orthodontics by way of extensive restorative dental work rarely improves the bite the way real orthodontics does and can be quite costly. It isn't unusual for a large restorative case to cost between $20,000 and $30,000.

Pros

- This method can quickly restore worn, broken, or discolored teeth.
- Work can be done in weeks instead of months or years.

Cons

- It is typically by far the most expensive of all options.
- It requires grinding down teeth and replacing them with porcelain.
- It requires several replacements throughout your lifetime.
- It doesn't typically correct the bite the way traditional orthodontics does.

Accelerated orthodontics. For many people, the time spent in orthodontic treatment is actually more important than how noticeable the braces are. Maybe you or your child is getting married in a year or less, and you want your new smile by then. By combining state-of-the-art advancements in orthodontic technology with advanced bone modulation, we can now complete almost all treatment safely and effectively in under a year, and many in just four to six months. Plus, you can use clear braces with these techniques. For more information on accelerated orthodontics, flip ahead to the next chapter, "Accelerated Treatment," or visit www.Brasik.com.

Beware of catchy brand names and too-good-to-be-true claims of faster treatment. Many companies imply in their names that their braces work better and faster than traditional orthodontics. Most of the difference in these techniques simply boils down to marketing. More sizzle than steak, as the expression goes. The names sound interesting, but commonly these procedures are offered by general dentists, not orthodontists. Delivering excellent outcomes in under a year is *very* complicated and requires a very high level of orthodontic skill and knowledge. Be very careful, and do your homework before choosing treatments promising fast tooth movements or the ability to finish braces in five to six months.

Pros

- This can be a great way to achieve high-quality treatment in a fraction of the time.

Cons

- Brand names and marketing can be misleading, and you may not be getting what you think you are getting.

Contemporary orthodontic treatment offers more options than ever before for those looking to avoid metal braces. I have provided a brief summary of the different choices for you here, but keep in mind that every individual is unique and requires a customized treatment plan from a well-trained orthodontist for the best results. Our office would be glad to schedule a free consultation for anyone looking for details specific to his or her own needs.

Accelerating Treatment

He can run faster than Severus Snape confronted with shampoo!

—J. K. Rowling

Accelerating treatment is one topic I have been very interested in throughout my career. This stuff is not Orthodontics 101. It's very advanced. (Warning: this chapter is a bit more technical than the others.) Accelerating orthodontic treatment safely and reliably is very complicated and is not within the skill set of most clinicians. If someone promises you treatment in under eight months—especially if that someone is not an orthodontist—be wary. There are a lot of orthodontic products with misleading names that make promises that cannot be kept. I have studied all the available options, participated in several clinical trials, taken courses from pioneers in the field, and lectured extensively on the topic around the world, so I know a thing or two about this area of expertise.

Accelerated treatments fall into four basic categories: mental, mechanical, digital, and physiological.

Mental. The most common and easiest way to faster treatment is to avoid making treatment go slower unnecessarily. If this sounds simple and intuitive, that's because it is. In far too many instances, the recommended "correct" time to begin orthodontic treatment is when the patient is in the office with a checkbook out. Having the proper starting point minimizes the amount of time you spend in braces and maximizes the amount of productive work the doctor can do at each adjustment visit. Many times, if treatment is started before all the baby teeth have fallen out (or at another premature time), treatment will be unnecessarily delayed, and more of the patient's time than necessary will be spent in braces. So in many instances the way to make treatment take less time is to wait awhile before starting treatment.

We have seen that there can be indications for starting treatment in a seven- to ten-year-old patient, but this should be limited to complicated cases involving problems with jaw growth, tooth growth, or development. Ideally, treatment in the first phase is limited to one year or less. Limiting phase-one treatment to that time span is not always possible but should always be the goal, as future treatment will be necessary to finalize the bite and the smile once the remaining permanent teeth have come in.

There are also indications to start treatment in eleven- to thirteen-year-old patients when the permanent teeth are not all the way in. These include blocked out or impacted teeth, significant overbite, or significant social concerns due to very misaligned teeth. However, many times, treatment is started earlier than is best for the patient just to get it "sold." Beware of starting treatment without a good reason on someone over ten years old who has not lost all of his or her baby teeth. Starting too early could unnecessarily prolong treatment and lead to months or years of extra braces, increased risk of tooth decay, and many unneeded trips to the orthodontist.

Mechanical. Mechanical acceleration can be done with a particular brace type called a self-ligating brace. Braces consist of two parts: the brace that attaches to the tooth and the wire. With traditional braces, the wire and brace are held together by small wires or elastic rubber bands. These wires or rubber bands, called *ligatures*, increase the friction between the brace and wire. Increased friction equals increased force necessary to move the teeth and therefore increased inflammation in the area.

People often ask me if there are risks with "moving the teeth too fast." The answer, surprisingly, is no. We have found, however, that there *are* increased risks from pushing too hard on a tooth. Orthodontics is an old boys' network, in which most of the doctors before the late eighties and early nineties were men. Like typical men (as I can attest, since I am male) we thought that to move the tooth faster and better, we should push *harder*. (I can hear all the ladies out there saying, "Typical!" Yes, I know.) As it turns out, the harder you push on a tooth, the more the tooth *resists* movement. The increased pressure causes increased inflammation around the tooth, which can lead to lots of unwanted side effects: increased gum problems, increased risk of root shortening, increased pain associated with tooth movement, and markedly *slower* tooth movement.

The self-ligating brace doesn't need the little wire or elastic ligature. It has a small built-in door that holds the brace and the wire together. Since this door does not apply much pressure to the wire, the wire can slide through the braces much more easily, and the entire system has exponentially less friction involved. You remember—friction is what causes you to get rug burn when you slide across a carpet. Friction is an increased resistance to sliding.

There are two main types of self-ligating brackets: active and passive. The differences in these types are discussed below.

Passive self-ligation. The easiest way to visualize how a passive self-ligating brace works is to imagine parking a car in a garage. The garage is the brace, and the car is the wire. The garage door is the small door in the brace. The car pulls into the garage, and the garage door shuts. If the car were placed in neutral and given a gentle push backward, the garage door would prevent it from rolling out. However, the garage door does not actively push on the bumper of the car to keep it in. This is exactly how a passive bracket works. You put the wire into the bracket, and the door keeps the wire from popping out.

Currently, my favorite style of brace is passive self-ligating. The popular brands are Damon System (the kind I use and prefer), Insignia (a customized Damon System brace we also use and will get to in the next section), Time, Carriere, Lotus, Empower, and a handful of others. Dr. Dwight Damon invented the Damon System bracket, and, in my opinion, he revolutionized the way orthodontic patients are treated. I have personally treated over seven thousand patients with the Damon System and have been thrilled with the quality and consistency of the results.

Because of the decreased friction and force necessary to move teeth, we are now able to move teeth in a healthier and safer way that is more comfortable for the patient. In addition, the bone that houses the teeth (the alveolar bone) reacts much more favorably to lighter forces, allowing faster tooth movement. It also drastically decreases the number of permanent-tooth extractions necessary to achieve beautifully straight teeth and an ideal bite. There were times when over 60 percent of all orthodontic cases required removal of at least two permanent teeth. In the United States today, over 35 percent of all patients are still being required to have permanent-tooth extractions. In our office and many others using the Damon System, less than 1 percent of patients require tooth extraction. This is an *incredible* change in treatment style that yields superior results with shorter treatment times. So, again, if you are given an opinion that permanent teeth should be removed, you may want to consider a second opinion. We are regularly able to help our patients avoid extractions, even when other doctors have recommended them.

Active self-ligation. Back to our garage example. Imagine that this time, the garage door had a little spring mechanism that made it apply pressure to the bumper of the car to keep it inside. This is the concept behind *active* self-ligation. The brace's door acts as a spring and puts pressure on the wire to keep it inside the braces. This raises the friction involved in the braces system; however, far less friction is involved than in traditional braces that require ligatures. Currently the main active self-ligating brackets are SPEED, Innovation, Innovation-C, Victory, Prodigy, and a handful of others. Most active self-ligating braces are, in my opinion, quality braces that are far superior to traditional ones. But every doctor has to pick one style, and I prefer the passive version.

Digital. As with everything else in today's world, the role computers play in orthodontics is ever increasing. The braces I've mentioned above are very sophisticated and require very specialized and complicated manufacturing and design processes. They are, however, built for the average person using "average" math. Each tooth has an individual brace that is built for the average size, shape, and such for that particular tooth. The upper-right central incisor has a slightly different brace from that of the upper-left central incisor, and so on.

Exciting new technology allows us to not only build braces for the "average" person but also individually customize each brace for each person based on the sizes and shapes of his or her teeth (not the average tooth) as well as to calculate the math required to move each individual tooth ideally. It's powered by really complicated, fancy math based on sophisticated algorithms.

There are four main players in the digitally customized orthodontic space:

1. **Invisalign**: Invisalign's aligners are digitally customized. They are worn all the time except for sleeping and eating (typically more than twenty hours per day). Each aligner (also called a tray) is slightly different from the previous. When worn in

order, they gradually and comfortably align the teeth. I've discussed Invisalign in greater detail in Chapter 6.

2. **Insignia**: Insignia is a digitally customized version of a passive self-ligating bracket (specifically the Damon bracket). Rather than using identical sets of braces on every patient, it is now possible to individually customize the entire set of brackets and wires for each person. Individual customization allows the same result (in some cases a better one) in fewer visits. As each person's teeth are of different sizes and shapes and the math behind moving each tooth is slightly different, the computer is used to customize treatments. This is the orthodontic equivalent to taking a direct flight instead of a connecting flight. The plane doesn't fly any faster (the teeth don't move any faster), but by going straight to its intended destination without wasted movement, a time savings is created by eliminating several adjustment visits at the end. Insignia is perfect for the person who needs braces with time being of the essence. He or she wants to be in and out of treatment as quickly as possible, in as few trips into the office as possible. My personal favorite in digital customization is Insignia because both the braces and the wires are customized. I was part of the original clinical trials for Insignia and

have treated over fifteen hundred patients with it to date. I have lectured around the world on digital customization of orthodontic treatment.

3. **SureSmile**: SureSmile is the third major player in today's digitally customized orthodontics space. SureSmile is a digitally customized wire technology by which the teeth—with the braces already on—are scanned into a computer, and a robot bends a series of wires to move the teeth into the perfect position. As robots can be more precise than even the most highly trained orthodontist, the adjustment phase of treatment proceeds more quickly and with fewer adjustments. SureSmile works with any bracket system and is a nice way to accelerate treatment. As with any accelerated treatment modality, there is a significant cost involved in using SureSmile, so be prepared to spend a little extra for the technology. SureSmile does not have customized braces but does have customized wires and was the first real player in the digital orthodontic treatment market.

4. **Incognito**: The other player worth mentioning is Incognito, a customized type of lingual braces (braces on the inside of the teeth). Lingual braces are most popular in other countries (especially Europe) and also in some big metropolitan areas in the United States, and with certain models, celebrities, and CEOs who absolutely cannot have

visible braces or aligners. The biggest pro for lingual braces, as discussed earlier, is the improved aesthetics during treatment. But as Invisalign has improved, the demand for lingual braces has decreased. However, digital technology is in the early stages of creating customized lingual braces, which may create a renaissance for them. Incognito is the first major player here. Be sure to look into it if you are considering this option, as more comfortable and less expensive treatments may soon be available to give a faster, better, and more affordable result.

Most digital products are also enhanced by the addition of digital intraoral scanners. Scanners now come in a variety of shapes, sizes, and manufactures, but their basic general function is to take three-dimensional pictures of your teeth and upload them to the computer. The computer can then use these images to build really cool 3-D stuff.

Digital scanners take the place of those yucky, bad-tasting impressions (dental molds) that make you gag. Every orthodontist and orthodontic worker has been thrown up on several times in the process of taking dental impressions. We don't like it when our patients throw up on us (and our patients *really* don't like it). Amazingly, technology has made the necessity of impressions obsolete.

However, although the technology is cool and is becoming more and more affordable, most offices have not totally eliminated impressions because they can be quick, easy, and cheaper for some procedures. However, an up-to-date office should be able to offer you impressionless orthodontic treatment. So, if avoiding impressions is very important to you, be sure to ask if scanning is possible!

Physiological. The area of orthodontics garnering a ton of current attention is physiologic orthodontic acceleration. This refers to a process of significantly altering the local physiology to allow faster tooth movement—think of using rocket fuel in place of regular fuel in your car. Also remember that rocket fuel costs more than regular gas; likewise, making teeth move significantly faster typically yields an increase in treatment cost. However, there are many people who would gladly give a little more money in exchange for dramatically faster tooth movement—hence the explosion in research and the products surrounding physiologic modification.

Physiologic modification alters the cellular processes in the areas around your teeth to speed the rate of tooth movement. Over the past several years, new products for this have emerged, and many more are currently in development or clinical trials. There are several different ways to make teeth move faster, so there are several companies with products in this space. It is important to emphasize that none of these modalities work without orthodontic pressure on the teeth (braces or aligners).

The following are some of the most popular accelerated modalities available today:

1. **Mechanical pulsation**. The biggest products in the area of mechanical pulsation are called AcceleDent and VibraPro 5. However, others will shortly be joining the market. They are hands-free devices with a vibrating mouthpiece that you bite on, typically for ten or twenty minutes. Mechanical pulsation works by applying a light vibrational force to your teeth and jaws that makes the cells around the teeth that are responsible for tooth movement (osteoclasts) work at a higher rate. This technology was first developed by orthopedic surgeons, who found that applying vibration to bone fractures caused them to heal faster. It has also been adapted for treating women who have osteoporosis. Standing on special vibrating scales—again, typically for twenty minutes—has been shown to improve their bone density. Mechanical pulsation devices appear to work particularly well with aligners. Another interesting side benefit of mechanical pulsation is a dramatic reduction in tooth soreness. The vibrational forces decrease some of the things that make teeth sore during orthodontics, and patients

report a dramatic reduction in tooth pain—with many reporting no discomfort at all. According to current research, mechanical pulsation can speed treatment by as much as 30 percent.

2. **Photobiomodulation**. Photobiomodulation, or PBM, is the most recent of the players in the area of physiologic acceleration, in the form of a product called OrthoPulse. OrthoPulse delivers a series of LED light pulses to the area around the gums, increasing blood flow locally. It is thought that the increased blood flow will allow teeth to move faster. The device is similar to an AcceleDent, but it lights up instead of vibrating. Using this product is completely painless; however, it does not seem to have the advantage of decreasing tooth pain. With research available today, it appears that PBM/OrthoPulse is capable of 30 to 40 percent reduction in treatment time; however, more research is needed, as OrthoPulse is very new to the market.

3. **Corticotomy**. Corticotomy is the process of making small, minimally invasive cuts in the bone around the teeth. They cause the bone there to think it is injured, so the body sends a series of healing cells to the area. These cells, in combination with orthodontic pressure on the teeth, create the fastest tooth-moving environment we have found in orthodontics to date. Corticotomy by itself does not create tooth movement—you

still need braces or aligners. However, it allows braces or aligners to work much faster. Of the physiological accelerants, corticotomy has been around the longest and is the most well-researched technique. There are three different corticotomy techniques in practice today:

a. **Wilckodontics**. The Wilckodontic technique was popularized by two doctors from Pennsylvania with the last name Wilcko. This is the most invasive of the three corticotomy techniques. In my area, it can run from $4,000 to $6,000 on top of the cost of the orthodontics. It requires a long surgical procedure that includes stitches and bone grafting. The procedure itself takes three or four hours and is typically done at an oral surgeon's or periodontist's office. Current research indicates that the Wilckodontic technique yields the fastest tooth movement and that its enhanced effect can last the longest—up to eight or nine months after the procedure. It is also the most sensitive of the corticotomy techniques. Definitely do some research if you are considering this technique. An experienced combination of orthodontist and surgeon are critical for success. I have personally treated several Wilckodontic cases in under five months, and they would have taken twenty-four months with traditional orthodontic techniques.

b. **Piezocision**. Piezocision works similarly to the Wilckodontic technique, except it typically requires no stitches or bone grafting. This technique may overtake Wilckodontics due to its relative advantages. The teeth move nearly as fast as with Wilckodontics but do so with a much less invasive procedure that is typically completed in less than an hour, and people are usually able to go back to work or school the next day. Because it is easier and less time-intensive than Wilckodontics, piezocision is also usually significantly less expensive (around $2,500 in my area). It does wear off after about six to eight months, so longer or more complicated orthodontic treatments may require reactivation with another piezocision procedure. My wife was actually treated with a combination of Insignia and piezocision, and her treatment was completed in five months, with a beautiful result. She has recommended this combination procedure to several of her friends.

c. **Micro-osteoperforation (MOP).** MOP has been popularized by a product called Propel. The Propel device creates small punctures in the bone around the teeth, creating acceleration of tooth movement. This is the least invasive corticotomy technique and is typically done in the orthodontic office, not by a surgeon. Since no second professional is needed, Propel treatments are also typically the least expensive. In my area, they run in the $1,000 range. (Remember that these prices are merely ranges and are *in addition* to the normal fees charged for orthodontics.) Propel is often done using only topical anesthesia, a gel-based numbing agent applied to the gums with a Q-tip. (Read: no shots!) Propel is also relatively painless and requires no downtime from work or school. It accelerates tooth movement for only about twelve weeks, so many reactivations are usually necessary. However, due to its ease, it only takes a small amount of additional time. Some doctors charge per activation for Propel, and others charge a flat fee that covers all necessary activations. Make sure you understand the pricing before you agree to Propel treatments.

Accelerated orthodontics is not a simple topic, and describing it in lay terms in a book for nonprofessionals is no easy task. This chapter is certainly not meant to be a complete guide but to inform you of the main techniques being used today to make teeth move faster. Please ask your orthodontist about these techniques if you are interested in them.

Last, beware of products marketed based on their speed or their inexpensive cost. Accelerating tooth movement is tricky business, even for very experienced specialists and surgeons. A number of products are limited in what they can do but are marketed as fast, cheap, and available in your general dentist's office. These offerings tend to correct front alignment but not the bite, and they can wind up causing more harm than good. We retreat many patients in our offices who have wasted their time, energy, and money on products that offer a too-good-to-be-true result. Remember to do your research before selecting an orthodontic provider so that your or your family's treatments have the highest chance of success. Use the information I've given you to ask educated questions of your prospective providers.

How to Make Orthodontic Treatment Affordable

If you don't go after what you want, you'll never have it. If you don't ask, the answer is always no. If you don't step forward, you're always in the same place.

—Nora Roberts

Investing in orthodontic treatment for you or your loved one is an investment in your health, an investment in self-confidence, and an investment in the future. However, buying orthodontics is a significant investment. It is not like buying a gallon of milk. Careful consideration and research is necessary before choosing who will do your treatment. So once you've done that and have decided on your orthodontic provider, it would be nice if you had some tricks to save money where possible.

FLEXIBLE SPENDING AND HEALTH SAVINGS ACCOUNTS

Flexible spending accounts (FSAs) and health savings accounts (HSAs) allow you to use pretax dollars for treatment.

Many FSAs let you put up to $2,500 per year toward qualified health-care expenses, which include orthodontics. With HSA accounts, you may be able to pay for the entire treatment pretax, as HSA accounts allow larger balances. HSA accounts do not reset every year the way FSA accounts do (confusing, I know). Either type of account is a significant tax advantage and can be the most powerful way to save money on your orthodontic treatment. Make sure you pay attention to your company's deadlines if you plan to use money from an FSA. Most companies require you to let them know ahead of time as well as how much you would like to set aside in the account. Also pay attention to enrollment periods: most companies allow you to enroll in either November or June, and failing to sign up in time could cost you significantly more in after-tax dollars to pay for your treatment. Again, most orthodontists offer free consultations, so be sure to get an orthodontic exam before the deadline to register for your flex account.

INSURANCE

If you have orthodontic insurance, congratulations! Approximately 50 percent of those seeking orthodontic treatment do not have that kind of coverage. Make sure to check what type of insurance your employer offers. Many have different options for orthodontic coverage. Some insurance policies also require a one-year waiting period, so you may have to sign up now for benefits next year. If you or a family member may be interested in orthodontics in the future, check with your insurance supplier to make sure you get the most benefit from your insurance.

Also, a common misconception is that you can only see an in-network orthodontist. False! For almost all orthodontic insurance, you will still get the same insurance benefit regardless of whether you see an in-network doctor or not. An orthodontist should provide you with a complimentary benefits check.

ASK FOR FLEXIBLE FINANCING

Most offices will offer you several options to pay for treatment. Typically, if you pay in full, you'll save a certain percentage. You can also make a down payment and take on one to two years of monthly payments. Or you can opt for an extended financing plan, but watch for hidden fees or surprise charges if you miss a payment. You shouldn't need to pay higher than a 7 or 8 percent APR for an extended (over twenty-four month) payment plan. You should also have the option for shorter payment plans with a 0 percent APR. Companies like OrthoFi are helping doctors make treatment more and more affordable for patients by giving them many different customized payment options.

WATCH FOR HIDDEN FEES

When comparing orthodontists' prices, look closely at the cheapest. Many offices offer low prices up front but hit you with fees later in treatment, making the total cost much higher. Fees for broken brackets, missed appointments, and cancellations and extra charges for retainers and the like can dramatically increase your total cost. Also beware of any office that charges additional monthly fees after a certain point. For example, many lower-priced offices will charge extra if treatment extends beyond twenty-four months—creating an incentive for them to keep your braces on longer. This is tricky business. Any time a healthcare provider appears disingenuous or deceptive in any way, be wary.

If you opt to use Invisalign, be sure to ask if refinements are included. The original sets of aligners rarely ever get your teeth perfectly straight. One or more refinements are usually needed, in which a new mold or scan is taken for additional aligners. We anticipate these in all of our Invisalign treatments. Your quoted fee should include all refinements. If it doesn't, you will likely face the choice of a significant additional cost or an incomplete result!

Also, lower-cost offices typically use lower-cost materials. Braces can be purchased from third-world manufacturers for a fraction of the cost of American-made braces. But all braces are *not* created equal. Many cheap braces are made of cheap metals. As with costume jewelry, lower-grade metals are much more likely to create irritation and sensitivity in patients. Higher-quality metals used in higher-quality braces are safer and less likely to create reactions or sensitivities.

Using a cheaper brace often leads to months or years in longer treatment and ten or fifteen additional office visits. Would you pay a few hundred dollars extra to be done with your braces sooner and to have far fewer trips to the doctor?

Consider quality before selecting your orthodontist. Shopping for the cheapest orthodontic treatment in town may come with a significant hidden cost in dollars, time, comfort, and your ultimate results. I've given you information that should allow you to select an orthodontist who puts quality first and will provide affordable payment options.

Eleven Things Parents Should Consider When Choosing an Orthodontist

A genuine leader is not a searcher for consensus but a molder of consensus.

—Martin Luther King Jr.

Choosing the right doctor for your family's orthodontic treatment is more confusing than ever. This chapter is meant as a quick reference to help you be an informed orthodontic consumer. Researching different orthodontists, treatment options, types of braces, or whether a clear product like Invisalign is right for you or a loved one can be overwhelming, and making a wise decision can seem daunting. To help clarify the important questions, I have composed the following list. I hope you find it helpful.

1. IS THE DOCTOR A SPECIALIST IN ORTHODONTICS?

A general dentist (often referred to as a restorative or cosmetic dentist) is similar to a family doctor who provides excellent care for your well-being and aids in disease prevention and treatment. Dentists are great for check-ups, preventive care, fillings, and cosmetic procedures. Although all orthodontists are dentists, only about 6 percent of dentists are orthodontists. An orthodontist is a specialist who has two to three years of additional education and training beyond dental school and is an expert in designing smiles by gently straightening your teeth. Orthodontists are the experts at choosing your best treatment options. Whether you're considering clear aligners or traditional braces, an orthodontist has the training, experience, and treatment expertise to make sure you get your best smile.

2. WHEN SHOULD YOUR CHILD BE EVALUATED?

The American Association of Orthodontists recommends that all children be evaluated by age seven. People are often surprised that orthodontics can be done on children so young. Many children do not need treatment before age ten; however, some do have problems that are treated much better at a younger age. Such problems can become much harder to correct when the patient is older. The best results in these cases occur when treatment is divided into two phases. Phase one is shorter and helps with jaw growth, making space, and allowing for proper tooth development. Phase two is meant to perfect the smile and the bite. It is important to have your child screened early to find out if he or she has a condition that requires early treatment.

3. DOES THE OFFICE HAVE A GREAT REPUTATION?

Do your research! Check social media sites like Google Plus and Facebook to see what others are saying about the office you're considering. On Yelp, make sure to look at the filtered reviews. Yelp has historically prioritized certain reviews for pay, so use caution when evaluating the validity of Yelp reviews. Facebook and Google Plus tend to be more reliable: they allow all reviews to be posted visibly, and they are not influenced by payment. Ask your friends and neighbors what they have heard about local orthodontists. It may be worth your while to drive a little farther to get higher-quality treatment and better customer service.

4. DOES THE OFFICE TREAT ADULTS?

With the advent of clear aligners, more aesthetic braces, and accelerated treatment, more adults than ever are seeking straighter teeth. We have many parents of patients who choose to have orthodontics for themselves as well. In our office, 20 percent of our patients are adults, and we have treated several patients in their eighties. Yes, I said *eighties*. We have yet to find anyone who is "too old" for treatment. It's never too late to have a beautiful, healthy smile. Treating adults, however, is different from treating growing children. Adults often have more dental restorations (fillings, crowns, and veneers) and gum problems and are no longer growing. These factors and more can complicate treatment. If you are an adult interested in orthodontics, you want someone experienced who devotes a significant part of his or her practice to adult treatment. Plus, many adults find enjoyment and bonding when having orthodontic treatment the same time as their child. So, if you are interested in a nicer smile consider being treated the same time as a loved one.

5. ARE THE RESULTS GUARANTEED?

Many years ago, orthodontists would tell patients that they could stop wearing retainers a year or two after braces were removed. Then teeth shifted, and the wisdom teeth were blamed. Now we know that to keep your teeth straight for a lifetime, you must wear retainers indefinitely, regardless of wisdom teeth or any other factor. But let's face it: not all people will do as instructed—dogs may eat retainers, or the retainers may be accidentally thrown away (or lost under the bed). In these cases, some teeth will shift, and, for some former patients, teeth will need to be restraightened. It is important to know what will happen and how much it will cost should you need to repeat braces at some point in the future.

6. IS THE QUOTED FEE ALL INCLUSIVE?

Many offices that seem to cost less at first have hidden fees that pop up during treatment. Broken braces (all patients—kids and adults—have broken braces from time to time), extra visits, treatment that extends past the estimated treatment time, canceled appointments, Invisalign refinements, retainers, and more can trigger hidden fees at many offices, raising the costs to much more than you bargained for. For Invisalign, make sure refinements are included! Be sure to read the fine print, and make sure that the fee you are quoted is the only fee you will pay. Don't be fooled by low treatment fees when the actual total out-the-door cost is much higher.

7. IS THE OFFICE UP TO DATE WITH THE LATEST TECHNOLOGY?

The world is changing rapidly. So, too, is the world of orthodontics. Advances in braces technology, clear aligners, and accelerated treatment make straightening teeth more comfortable, more efficient, faster, easier, and less noticeable than ever before. Braces can even be placed behind your teeth, but only if the orthodontist spends considerable time, energy, and effort to invest in learning and mastering the latest techniques. If any doctor suggests extractions, headgear, or more than two years of treatment, make sure to get another opinion.

8. ARE THERE AFFORDABLE PAYMENT OPTIONS?

Braces—even with the best doctors—can and should be affordable. Zero-down, no-interest payment plans should be available for those who can't afford a large down payment. Extended payment plans should be available to allow for lower monthly payments. For extended plans, you may need to pay a little interest. However, the rate should be low (think 5 or 6 percent), not high like that of a credit card. Also, if you use a third-party financing service (Care Credit, Springstone, or others), be careful of penalty interest. For example, many companies offer 0 percent financing, but if you miss a single payment, they pile on penalty charges of over 20 percent—of the entire cost of treatment. This takes the financing from 0 percent interest to over 20 percent, changing the total cost of treatment by hundreds or sometimes more than a thousand dollars. Be sure to read the fine print.

Be wary of shopping for rock-bottom prices. Many of the cheapest offices use outdated materials, braces bought from third-world countries, reused braces, or the hidden fees that don't present themselves until later in treatment (raising the total cost). Remember, you often get what you pay for. It may be worth paying a few extra dollars to ensure high-quality treatment. Orthodontics is an investment that should last a lifetime.

Also, many offices accept insurance, reducing the out-of-pocket expense. They also work with FSAs or HSAs that allow payments to be made pretax.

9. DOES THE OFFICE RUN EFFICIENTLY?

Unfortunately, your time is not as valuable to the medical community as it is to you. We all know that most doctors' waiting rooms are exactly that: a place where you wait. Your orthodontist should value your time and be prompt in both welcoming you to the visit and getting you out within your scheduled time. Your time is valuable, too.

10. DOES THE OFFICE SUPPORT THE COMMUNITY?

The community around an orthodontic office is what supports the practice. Therefore, it is not unreasonable to expect the office to support the community in return. And this doesn't mean just paying for marketing opportunities in local sports programs. The office should be committed to supporting local communities in a meaningful way, set an example for giving back to the children they treat, and provide treatment for underprivileged children in the area.

11. DOES THE OFFICE FEEL FUN?

Orthodontic treatment doesn't have to be a scary or unpleasant experience. It should be fun! Advances in orthodontic treatment make transforming your smile more comfortable than ever. Look for personal touches, fun contests, and rewards programs in an office to see how much it truly cares about making your child's (or your) experience special. Each visit should be something to smile about!

Choosing the right office and right treatment for you or your loved ones is a difficult decision, and the ever-growing number of options does not make choosing any easier. I hope that the information presented in this book is helpful to you as you seek a more healthy and beautiful smile.

To forward a digital copy of the final chapter of this book to friends and family, please direct them to www.OrthoQuestions.com.

If you know someone who would like to request a free copy of this book, please direct them to www.MadeInDetroitOrthoBook.com.

For more information about our practice, please visit www.MyAmazingSmile.com.

For more information about me or to ask me a question directly, please visit www.AskDrReynolds.com.

Made in the USA
Middletown, DE
30 January 2019